# Wine & Dine
## with New Hampshire

# *Wine & Dine*
## with New Hampshire

*Carla Snow, CSW*

Photographs by Brian Smestad :: Foreword by Jude Blake

Reed,
Come & enjoy the
wonderful world
of NH Wines!
*[signature]* 1.27.2011

Reed,
Enjoy the photographs
*[signature]*

### Blue Tree
PORTSMOUTH

First published in the United States in 2009
by Blue Tree, LLC
P.O. Box 148
Portsmouth, NH 03802

37 10 1

Printed in Hong Kong

Library of Congress
Cataloging-in-Publication Data
2009920995

Wine & Dine with New Hampshire
Carla Snow, CSW
Photographs by Brian Smestad
Foreword by Jude Blake

First edition, May 2009

ISBN-10: 0-9802245-8-6
ISBN-13: 978-0-9802245-8-0

For customer service, orders, and book projects:
Local 603.436.0831
Toll-Free 866.852.5357
Email sales@TheBlueTree.com

www.TheBlueTree.com

Blue Tree
AN ARTISTIC PUBLISHING COMPANY

# *Contents*

# *Foreword*

Switzerland and California—who would guess that they have much to do with the wineries of New Hampshire? But they do.

In 1973, I arrived on the campus of the University of New Hampshire in Durham. Having moved across the country and back again many times as a child, I found there a place I could call home. I put down roots—deep roots, because for me, at the age of seventeen, four years in one locale was a long stay. I loved the beauty of the Seacoast in the spring, the magnificent autumn vistas and colors, and the high mountains covered with winter snows. New Hampshire took hold of my soul.

My corporate marketing career carried me away again, across the country, and then around the world. I eventually landed in Switzerland, a small country that bears many similarities to New Hampshire. Both places are relatively small. Both are populated by fiercely independent people who would rather "live free or die" than succumb to governance by anyone other than themselves. They both share an economic base that was historically agricultural but is now driven by tourism and high-tech and entrepreneurial ventures.

While working in Switzerland, I needed something to fill my weekends. As a long time oenophile, I spent those days visiting the small wineries of the region. I struggled to speak a language I could barely discern, as *Schweizerdeutsch* is a medieval form of German, and a language that is spoken, not written. However, the language of wine and winemaking gave me common ground with the producers, and through my visits I learned to understand the difficulties that winemakers have to deal with. Like New Hampshire, northern Switzerland is a region where vines struggle to thrive and grapes struggle to ripen. The cool climate means short growing seasons and often turbulent weather. Rocky soil and hilly terrain make tending the grapes a labor by manual means, and small family-owned farms result in tiny output. All in all, it is a tough way to make a living. Yet those who choose to make wine demonstrate a passion and pride that can only be described as admirable.

When I left Switzerland in 2005, I moved to Northern California to run a small family-owned winery, now called Peter Paul Wines. (Like myself, Peter Paul is also rooted in New Hampshire, having grown up in the small town of Troy.) In California, winemaking is much easier. Napa and Sonoma Counties boast near-perfect weather and soil for grape growing, with fruit so rich and lush that the wine almost makes itself. Even in the Granite State, we have built a strong following for our vineyard-designated, single varietal Peter Paul Wines.

But while California wine country was a wonderful place to live and work, I still yearned for the cool, crisp autumn days of New England. On one such beautiful September day in 2007, I arrived in Portsmouth. Strolling through the charming colonial town that afternoon, a sign caught my

eye. It read, "New Hampshire wine tasting today." Following that calling, I entered a shop called Maine-ly New Hampshire. I asked about tasting New Hampshire wines and was presented with the Jewell Towne Vineyards Dry Riesling. With bright floral notes and crisp citrus and pear flavors, this wine was reminiscent of the beautiful Rieslings of northeastern Switzerland. It was an uncanny revelation for me.

Now intrigued by New Hampshire wines, a bottle of Maréchal Foch caught my eye. I had only seen wine from this hybrid red grape made in Switzerland, by my local producer in the small town of Neftenbach. Maréchal Foch is a hardy, early-ripening variety, with a medium structure and Burgundian characteristics, well suited for the cool climes of both Switzerland and New Hampshire. I mentioned the Swiss connection to the owner of the shop, Ken Smith, who proceeded to enlighten me with stories of these New Hampshire wines. He proudly told me that Maine-ly New Hampshire carries only wines made in-state, and he ships them throughout the country.

There are now twelve wineries producing wine in the state of New Hampshire. Wine was first produced here in the late 1960s, making the state a relative newcomer to the industry. New Hampshire will never rival California in terms of wine production, but the industry fits well within New Hampshire's agricultural roots and tourism trade. It is an industry still in its youth, with a bright future ahead. Yet it is New Hampshire's similarities to Swiss wine, winemaking, and independent spirit that I find most fascinating.

So what about that Maréchal Foch? It is now the most widely planted grape in the Granite State, and as the vines age, the wines made from these grapes will achieve even higher quality. Some friends and I recently conducted a tasting of New Hampshire and Swiss Maréchal Foch from the 2005 vintage. While different, both wines are absolutely delicious, full of bright cherry and plum notes, reminiscent of a fine quality Beaujolais.

Indeed, it was the Maréchal Foch that was responsible for my own re-rooting in New Hampshire. The sign that read, "New Hampshire wine tasting today" pulled me into a shop on Deer Street. In that shop, with a taste of wine, I discovered that while I had left New Hampshire, New Hampshire never left me.

—Jude Blake
*Peter Paul Wines*
*Larkspur, California, and Portsmouth, New Hampshire*

# Introduction

In today's society, many of us are concerned about the health of the environment, as well as the health of our family and friends. We've become more conscious of eating locally, to ensure that we are using the freshest organically grown products. Local suppliers also help reduce our carbon footprint.

Well, I am an advocate for "drinking locally," too. Drinking wine, that is. New Hampshire vineyards have premium quality grapes and fruit, sophisticated winemaking equipment, and tremendously talented winemakers who are producing some extraordinary wines. These wines are widely available at our local stores, restaurants, and, of course, directly from the vineyards.

Wine is my passion. I live it, breathe it, study it, and enjoy sharing it with others. I have made it my mission to learn about and experiment with many varieties of wine, all around the world. Over the years, I have had the privilege of raising my glass with many successful wine professionals and winemakers. I was thrilled to have the opportunity to study at the prestigious Le Cordon Bleu in Australia, where I earned both Culinary and Sommelier Certificates. It was truly an honor to spend time with some of the most experienced, knowledgeable people in the industry, and they encouraged me to keep exploring and sampling new things.

From there, I spent time in Bordeaux and the Rhône, to apprentice with the world's best winemakers. I gained valuable hands-on experience producing top-quality wine and selecting the right wines for specific occasions. And, yes, I did quite a bit of wine tasting as well.

But as exciting as it was to tour the globe sampling a variety of spectacular wines, I always knew I would return home to my native state, New Hampshire. When I arrived in 2003, I began working with a local wine importer and distributor, who helped me further extend my knowledge of wines. By that point, I had tasted the world's most luxurious wines, and I was truly impressed with the exceptional quality of wines produced right here at home.

I continued my studies in courses like the Bordeaux educators certification, and became an involved member of the Society of Wine Educators, as New Hampshire's first female Certified Specialist of Wine (CSW).

Since 2006, I've been selecting wines for New Hampshire's finest restaurants and stores; I often choose bottles from fantastic local vineyards, such as Jewell Towne Vineyards, Candia Vineyards, LaBelle Winery, Farnum Hill Cider, Piscassic Winery, Zorvino Vineyards, and Flag Hill Winery and Distillery. I consider New Hampshire wines to be on par with those from more well-known wine producing regions, and I am delighted to be able to spotlight these selections.

New Hampshire wines are not to be compared to those of Napa Valley; they are excellent for what they are and for what New Hampshire has to offer. New Hampshire does well with making wines with apples, grapes, and honey. The most widely grown grape varieties are Maréchal Foch and Seyval, and the most widely used fruits are berries and apples.

New Hampshire is known for many things—its beautiful lakes, magnificent skiing, and quaint little towns—but its wines have long been overlooked. In this book, I spill the secrets of New Hampshire's wines, sharing the hidden gems of New Hampshire's vineyards, and encouraging people to sample the delicious offerings of my home state.

The wine industry in New Hampshire started with John and Lucille Canepa of Laconia. They were the pioneers when they planted vines on their land on Governor's Island in 1965. They bought a farm near Belmont, in 1968, and created White Mountain Vineyards in time for the crush in 1969. By the early 1970s, approximately two hundred acres of French hybrid grapes were being grown in New Hampshire. The Canepas sold White Mountain Vineyards in 1984, and it was eventually renamed the New Hampshire Winery when it moved to Henniker, in the summer of 1990. When Bill Damour bought the winery, he made 30,000 gallons of wine, although only two of the wines were 100 percent New Hampshire wines. Unfortunately, due to financial problems, the winery was out of business by 1995. In 1994, Jewell Towne Vineyards, owned by Peter and Brenda Oldak, became the first of today's existing New Hampshire wineries to survive, and is still in operation today, followed closely by Flag Hill, owned by Frank W. Reinhold.

Hybridization made grape growing possible in cooler regions such as New Hampshire. "First were the French-American hybrids, originally developed in France in the late 1800s, and then more recently the hybrids developed at the American and Canadian University Agricultural Extensions and Field Stations. The hybrids are varieties of grape which are more cold hardy than their European vinifera parents, more disease resistant," explains Peter Oldak at Jewell Towne Vineyards, president of the New Hampshire Winery Association. "The second significant advance relates to the increased knowledge about viticulture and the relationships between trellising vines, sun exposure, soil, vine nutrition, pest management, and matching the right vine to the right climate and site."

There were actually twelve licensed wineries in New Hampshire as of 2006, although I have only focused on seven of them for this book. It was important that the winery already have a reputation and wines that were readily available before featuring them, and I would expect a revised edition of this book in a few years.

I talk to many people through my work, hobbies, and charitable endeavors, and often the subject turns to wine. When I ask them where their preferred wines come from, they usually say France, Italy, Australia, or California. When I ask them whether they have tried the wide variety of tasty wines that are produced right here in New Hampshire, they are surprised to hear that I consider our local wines to be as impressive as those bottled in more famous wine-producing regions. Many people have not even considered trying the extensive variety of wines available here.

I suggest that people clear their minds and palates of everything they know about wine, start from scratch, and be prepared to experience a new world. New Hampshire wines are unique and special. Some critics use the term "foxy" when describing wines from New Hampshire. This term refers to the grapey flavors of wines made from the native American species *Vitis labrusca*, and is an accurate descriptor for some wines.

I understand that many people are intimidated by wines and often stand nervously in front of the displays at their local liquor store, wine shop, or grocery store, gazing at the vast number of options in the marketplace today. Many people have told me that they are concerned about selecting the "right" wine, and are worried about following all of the wine-pairing rules. Their apprehension increases when they are trying to pick a special bottle to serve at an important dinner party or give as a gift to a top client, and so forth.

Food and wine pairing is 99 percent preference and 1 percent science. There are contrasting pairings and complementary pairings. Try to match the weight of the food with the weight of the wine. Think in terms of dairy; does the wine feel like skim milk, whole milk, or cream? The heavier the food is, the heavier the wine should be. When people ask me what they should drink with a steak dinner or a lighter meal like fish, I often tell them to try a Candia Vineyards Classic Cab with the steak, and a crisp Jewell Towne Cayuga White with the fish. A LaBelle Winery Dry Apple Sangria would be a great choice for a get-together with girlfriends, served with light snacks. For a romantic date night, try Flag Hill's North River Port with chocolates. For a holiday meal, a must-have is Farnum Hill's Semi-Dry Cider, and Jewell Towne's Léon Millot. A mead from Piscassic Pond Winery is good for mellowing out when you get home from a crazy day at the office.

I have written this book to raise awareness of these local treasures from my home state, and I enthusiastically encourage people to sample the variety of delicious wines available throughout New Hampshire. I explore the best of the wines from each winery. Three wines from each winery are presented with recipes that either use the wine as an ingredient or as a perfect pairing.

May you always enjoy great wine with great friends!

—Carla Snow, CSW

# Candia Vineyards

There is a definite New Hampshire charm surrounding financial-analyst-turned-winemaker Bob Dabrowski, owner of Candia Vineyards. Tired of crunching numbers, he decided to focus on his true passion: winemaking. Dabrowski has always loved wine and knew he would eventually run his own vineyard.

In 1981, he embraced winemaking as a hobby and happily made his first several bottles. Wanting to take things a step further, he planted his first grapes—Léon Millot. Distribution began in 2005, with fewer than one thousand bottles. Three years later, his business had grown significantly, producing more than 6,500 bottles.

Candia Vineyards grows a variety of delicious grapes on-site, including Frontenac, Frontenac Gris, La Crescent, La Crosse, Diamond, Maréchal Foch, Léon Millot, Marquette, and Noiret. Although Candia does not grow all of the grapes for the wine they produce, the other grapes used do come from within the United States—primarily New York and California.

Candia Vineyards has a tasting room in the basement in Candia, and as a nod to Bob's financial background, the wines are kept in a room with a bank vault door. During tastings, Bob and his team animatedly tell the story behind each wine, showcasing their knowledge of winemaking. Bob's enthusiasm for wines is evident—his eyes light up as he describes each grape and bottle.

When tasting wines, it is standard to taste from white to red, from dry to sweet, which allows the palate to experience each of the different flavors without being overwhelmed. Bob typically starts tastings with red wines, however, since Candia's whites tend to be on the sweet side. Since Bob understands the importance of food and wine pairing, he provides helpful advice regarding the types of food that would be most appropriate to serve with the vineyard's different varietals.

Candia Vineyards offers delicious wines with eye-catching artwork on the labels. Once the team thinks of a concept for a label, they work collaboratively with local artist Scott Beedle to create a design. The labels, which are mostly black and white, are beautiful and distinctive. The "Presidential Reds" created for the 2008 Presidential campaign were hugely popular, due in part to their visual wit. Of course, they were also delicious.

Candia Vineyards is located in a residential area of Candia, New Hampshire, on some of the state's oldest farmland. Bob and his team take great pride in the rich tradition of New Hampshire farming, and are dedicated to preserving the area's agricultural history and crafting only the highest-quality products.

### Frontenac

A stunning French hybrid. This variety can be used for port, or made into a lighter wine, as Bob has done. It needs the heat of our summers to ripen properly, and can survive extreme weather conditions, making it a good variety to grow in New Hampshire. This type of grape is used extensively in Minnesota, where it is bred at the University of Minnesota. The wine tastes of blackberry and boysenberry and is so fresh and clear, it is like fruit just picked from the vine. It has a medium acid with light to medium body (the mouthfeel of two percent milk).

### Noiret

Candia Vineyards was the first in New Hampshire to grow this grape, which has a complex background. Bred at Cornell University, it is a hybrid red wine grape that combines Chancellor Cross and Steuben. It is a dry, intense, and cold-hardy grape that grows very successfully in New England. This wine contains lots of blueberry notes, with moderate acid and a touch of oak, and is fruity but not sweet.

### Good King Robert's Red

Made with a blend of Cabernet grapes and a few other "field blends." More plummy fruit jam and a black cherry finish. Everyone's favorite.

### Classic Cab

This wine is made from California Cabernet fruit, and tastes like a California Cab but is made in New Hampshire. The juicy flavor is laced with mocha and tobacco. Great tannins make it a perfect wine to pair with foods such as rib eye or chocolate.

### Diamond

Known as the first quality dry wine produced in the United States from Labrusca grapes after they were hybridized by Jacob Moore of Brighton, New York, in 1885. This wine definitely has the "foxy" nose that is typical of Labrusca grapes. Candia Vineyards makes this in a fruity semisweet style that is fun to sip.

### La Crescent

Simply delicious! Candia Vineyards is the first in New Hampshire to produce this varietal. It was introduced in 2002 by the University of Minnesota. This wine has a Moscato-type nose of candied apricot, melon, papaya, and mango, with a lovely honey finish.

1 tablespoon grapeseed oil
Four 5- to 6-ounce rib-eye or top sirloin
    steaks, each about 1½ inches thick
3 tablespoons minced shallot
⅓ cup tawny port
⅔ cup Candia Vineyards Noiret
1 cup beef broth, low sodium if
    using canned
1½ teaspoons Dijon-style mustard
2 teaspoons balsamic vinegar
3 teaspoons fresh thyme, chopped
1 tablespoon unsalted butter, cold
Salt and pepper, to taste

SERVES 4

# Sirloin with Noiret Pan Sauce

Preheat the oven to 400°F. Line a baking pan with foil. Pat the steaks dry and season both sides with salt and pepper. In a heavy-bottomed skillet, heat the oil over moderately high heat until it is hot, but not smoking. Lay the steaks in the pan and sear for 2 minutes. Turn the steaks and sear on the other side for 2 minutes.

Remove the steaks and arrange them on the foil-lined baking pan. Place the pan in the preheated oven and cook for 8 minutes more for medium-rare. Transfer the steaks to a cutting board and cover with foil to keep warm.

To prepare the sauce, heat the pan used to sear the sirloin over low heat, and in the fat remaining in the pan cook the shallot, stirring until it is softened, about 2 minutes. Add the port and the Noiret and simmer the mixture until it is reduced by about two-thirds.

Add the beef broth and continue to simmer until the mixture is reduced by half. Add the mustard to the sauce and continue to simmer, whisking occasionally, for 2 minutes. Stir in the balsamic vinegar, thyme, and any juices that have accumulated on the cutting board from the steaks. Remove the pan from the heat, and whisk in the cold butter until it is melted and the sauce is glossy. Season with salt and pepper. Slice the steak into ¼-inch slices and serve with the sauce drizzled over the top.

1 pound (21-25) shrimp,
   deveined and peeled
2 tablespoons olive oil
1 small onion, sliced thin
4 garlic cloves, slivered
Pinch crushed red pepper
1 cup Candia Vineyards Diamond
1 pint grape tomatoes, halved
1 cup heavy cream
1 tablespoon orange zest, in long strips
1 tablespoon fresh rosemary, chopped
¼ cup fresh flat-leafed parsley, chopped
⅓ cup pine nuts, toasted
Salt and pepper, to taste
1 pound cooked pasta

Serves 4

Diamond

# Diamond Scampi

## with Fresh Pasta

In a large sauté pan, heat the onion and the oil over medium-low heat. Sauté until the onion is soft and translucent, about 5 to 7 minutes. Add the garlic and cook for an additional 2 minutes, stirring frequently. Add the shrimp and sauté for 1 to 2 minutes on each side.

Raise the heat to medium-high and add the wine. Simmer rapidly to reduce the wine by about one-third. Add the heavy cream and tomatoes and bring back to a simmer. Cook for about 3 minutes to thicken slightly. Add the crushed red pepper, orange zest, rosemary, and parsley and simmer for an additional 2 minutes to allow the flavors to combine.

Finish with toasted pine nuts and season with salt and pepper. Serve over pasta.

NOIRET PÂTÉ
2 cups Candia Vineyards Noiret
6 ounces semisweet chocolate
10 ounces bittersweet chocolate
½ cup heavy cream

CLASSIC CAB DESSERT SAUCE
2 cups Candia Vineyards Classic Cab
⅓ cup sugar
One 3-inch cinnamon stick
1 star anise pod (*optional*)
Pinch salt
1 tablespoon cornstarch mixed with
    1 tablespoon cold water
1 teaspoon grated lemon zest
1 teaspoon fresh lemon juice

MAKES EIGHTEEN ½-INCH SLICES

# Noiret Pâté

## with Classic Cab Dessert Sauce

Line a small loaf pan, approximately 7 by 3 by 2 inches, with two strips of parchment paper, one down the middle and one along the sides. In a heavy-bottomed saucepan, bring the Noiret to a boil and reduce to 1 cup (this evaporates the water). Remove pan from heat.

Add both chocolates to the wine and let sit for 5 minutes. Stir the wine and melted chocolate with a whisk until smooth. Add the heavy cream and stir to combine. Pour into the loaf pan and refrigerate for 24 hours. To serve, allow the pâté to come to room temperature. Invert the loaf pan on a flat surface lined with parchment paper and remove the pan and parchment from the pâté. Slice the pâté with unflavored dental floss.

To make the dessert sauce, simmer the Classic Cab, sugar, cinnamon, star anise, and salt in a heavy-bottomed nonreactive saucepan over high heat until the liquid is reduced by half, about 5 minutes.

Stir the cornstarch mixture and add it to the simmering reduction. Stir the sauce as it thickens, for about 3 minutes. Remove from heat and stir in the lemon zest and juice and let sit for 2 minutes. Strain the sauce. Serve warm, or refrigerate for 4 hours and serve cold.

# Farnum Hill Ciders

When Stephen Wood started managing apple production at Poverty Lane Orchards in 1973, New England apples were widely sold along the East Coast, and as far away as England.

Back then, Poverty Lane Orchards had a reputation for growing high-quality Cortland and McIntosh apples which were carefully picked, inspected, and packed by hand. Steve bought the orchards in 1984, intending to continue the pick-your-own and wholesale apple business. However, grocery chains started wanting big, waxed fruit, promoting visual appeal over taste. New plantings and shipping technologies sent imported apples—Granny Smith, in particular—pouring up from the Southern Hemisphere into North American winter markets. The quality advantage of wholesale orchards in northern New England had begun to disappear.

Around that time, Steve and his wife, Louisa Spencer, visited England and noticed some unusual-looking orchards belonging to Bulmers Cider, the world's largest producer of fermented cider. Curious, Steve arranged to meet with Bertram Bulmer, then the managing director of the company. He learned that Bulmers used apple varieties that were inedible as fruit, good only for hard cider. To learn more, Steve made several trips through England's cider regions, studying many cidermakers and growers.

By the early 1990s, Poverty Lane Orchards was struggling. Demand for New England apples continued to diminish, with no turnaround in sight. Steve took cidermaking courses in England and began cutting down acres of his New England apple trees, making room for English and French cider varieties and restructuring his business.

Through trial and error, he learned to work with Farnum Hill's distinctive soil and weather conditions and figured out which apples would grow most effectively on his land. Following the English producers he knew best, Steve wanted to produce still hard cider exclusively, but his customers preferred sparkling cider. He honored their requests and learned to make delicious sparkling cider with his fruit. Now he declares that American ciders should be as individual as the ground they grow from.

Cider is fermented from apples, similar to the way wine is fermented from grapes. Most ciders are blended from apples that are high in sugars, tannins, and crisp, bracing malic acid. Unlike apples grown to eat, much cider fruit is gathered from the ground for optimum ripeness. The staff at Farnum Hill Ciders constantly test different apple varieties and combinations to produce the tastiest ciders.

Today, they make approximately two thousand cases of hard cider a year, and their cider has won rave reviews from the public and the media. Farnum Hill Ciders has been featured in such leading publications as *Wine Enthusiast*, *Food & Wine*, *The New York Times*, and *Martha Stewart Living*.

## Summer Cider
The name really suits this cider, which offsets the heat of summer. It is clean and refreshing, with just the right hint of apple sweetness. This cider, available only during the summer months, is something to look forward to. Do not chill this too much—or any of the ciders. To maximize the fruity flavors, the ideal serving temperature is about 55°F.

## Farmhouse
This is the lightest and least serious of the ciders. A clean, light "quaffing" cider, it perfectly balances sweet and bitter. This bottle has a crown cap like a beer bottle but is much less filling than beer and a lot more satisfying. Beer drinkers hesitant to move over to wine should give Farmhouse a try.

## Extra Dry
Like Farnum Hill's Semi-Dry, it is made from a range of late-harvest, difficult to grow apple varieties. Fermented as dry as it will go, this has lovely fruit with more earthiness than the Semi-Dry.

## Extra Dry Still
This cider has a full cork closure, so be sure to have a corkscrew handy. This is wonderfully aromatic, with a great balance of fruit and acidity. Excellent with meals.

## Semi-Dry
This is Farnum Hill's most popular cider and is perfect for people trying cider for the first time. It makes a great apéritif with cheese or brunch. Don't let the "semi-dry" designation fool you—this is much less sweet than a semi-dry Champagne. This cider gently bubbles with tropical fruits and citrus on the nose.

## Kingston Black Reserve
The best cider to pair with food, this is what we serve at Thanksgiving. This is the only still at 8.5 percent alcohol. It has the mouthfeel of a Chardonnay, with low balanced acidity. It's made from the bittersharp Kingston Black apple, long treasured abroad as a single-variety cider fruit for its rare balance of tannin, sugar, and acid. They don't make much of this gem, so if you are lucky enough to find some, grab it!

## SHALLOT VINAIGRETTE

1 egg
¼ cup rice wine vinegar
½ cup sherry vinegar
1 tablespoon Dijon-style mustard
3 medium shallots, halved
1 garlic clove, whole
Salt and pepper, to taste
Light olive oil or blended oil

## SALAD

1 pound arugula (*preferably from a local farm, for the spiciness*)
4 ounces Tomme, sliced thin
3 ounces candied almonds
1 red pepper, roasted, cleaned, and sliced into ribbons

SERVES 4

Farmhouse Cider

# Arugula and Boggy Meadow Fiddlehead Tomme Salad

## with Shallot Vinaigrette and Crispy Almonds

In a blender, purée the egg, vinegars, shallot, garlic, pinch of salt and pepper, and mustard. Slowly drizzle in oil until the dressing is creamy. Taste, and adjust the seasoning.

In a bowl, toss the arugula with enough dressing to coat; taste again for seasoning. Divide among 4 plates and top with nuts, sliced cheese, and pepper strips. Serve with Farmhouse Cider.

Farmhouse Cider has a light but very rustic flavor, finishing a little herbaceous. With the spiciness of arugula and the muskiness of Tomme, it will be a joy on your palate.

1 Fuji apple, peeled and diced small
10 spines from a rosemary twig
   (*must be fresh*)
5 eggs
3½ ounces butter
1 cup water
1 teaspoon salt
Pinch sugar
1¼ cups all-purpose flour

MAKES 36

# Rosemary Apple Puffs

Preheat a conventional oven to 450°F (or a convection oven to 400°F). In a saucepot, bring the water, butter, salt, and sugar to a boil, stir in the flour, and use a rubber spatula or wooden spoon to stir. The mix will tighten; reduce the heat to medium and cook the mixture while stirring constantly for 2 to 3 minutes. Place the mixture in a mixing bowl with a paddle, run at medium speed, and drop in one egg at a time, adding the next after the previous egg has been incorporated. Continue until the final egg has been worked for 2 minutes. Add the rosemary and stir 1 more minute. Remove the bowl from the machine and with a wooden spoon or rubber spatula, fold in the apples.

Line a baking sheet with either a silpat or sprayed parchment paper. Using a breakfast or soup spoon, scoop batter about half the size of a ping pong ball. Drop the batter 3 inches apart, approximately 36 rounds to the pan. Bake in a 450°F conventional oven (no fan) for 12 minutes, then lower the heat to 300°F and bake for an additional 10 minutes. (When using a convection oven, bake for 7 minutes at 400°F, then reduce heat to 300°F and bake for an additional 7 minutes.) Remove from oven, allow to cool, then serve.

You may use these as a light dessert or starter. They make a great party hors d'oeuvre. Light and fruity calls for Summer Cider.

1 pork shoulder, 10 to 15 pounds, studded
    with 10 whole garlic cloves
3 medium onions, diced
12 garlic cloves, whole
2 pinches saffron
6 apples, cored and wedged (*Golden
    Delicious would be a good choice*)
½ pound currants
1 pound drained Spanish olives
    with pimento
½ bottle Farnum Hill Kingston Black
2 teaspoons cinnamon
½ bunch fresh oregano, chopped
1 orange, zest only
1 quart chicken stock (*or pork stock*)
Salt and pepper, to taste

SERVES 4

Kingston Black Reserve

# Braised Spanish Porketta

After studding the pork with garlic, truss it with twine to achieve a uniform shape. Season with salt and pepper.

Heat a large braising pan or rondeau with olive oil over medium heat; place the fatty portion of the "round" down into the hot oil. Allow to sear until golden-brown. Turn and brown all sides. On the final side, add the onions and garlic; allow to cook until the onions are translucent.

Add the olives, apples, and saffron and stir until you can smell the saffron. Add the cinnamon, currants, salt, pepper, orange zest, and Kingston Black and reduce by half. Add the chicken stock, bring to boil, and shut off the heat—your liquid content should only be halfway up the side of the round. Cover with parchment or a lid (when using a lid, remove it ¾ of the way through the cooking process).

Place the pan in a 300°F oven. The time may vary, but 3 to 4 hours is average for a 15-pound shoulder. Test doneness by trying to pull a piece off the edge; if it falls right off, it is finished. Remove from the oven and allow to rest 45 minutes. Remove from the pan. Reserve the liquid and braising mixture, remove the strings, and slice the pork thin.

Serve over yellow Spanish rice, mashed plantains, or alone. Top with liquid and accompaniments from the pan and serve with Kingston Black; its earthy backbone and medium tannins compliment the aromatics and hearty content of this dish.

# Flag Hill Winery

Reinhold Farm in Lee, New Hampshire, once a family-owned dairy farm with large herds of cattle and sheep, belonged to patriarch Frank Sr., whose son, Robert, managed the property. But in 1964, the family closed the farm and sold the livestock, and for the next twenty-one years, the property sat unused.

In 1985, Frank Jr., the youngest of the eight Reinhold children and a former nuclear operator in the Navy, took up residence on the property with his wife Linda. They planned their next career as grape-growers and winemakers, and changed the property's name to Flag Hill Farm.

Frank Jr. and Linda planted their first acre of grapes in 1990. The first harvest occurred in 1994; they sold all of their fruit to the New Hampshire Winery in Henniker. The 1995 harvest was processed, stored, and vintnered by Flag Hill. The following spring, Flag Hill Winery was established, producing five hundred cases, consisting of four types of wine. It also became New Hampshire's first working distillery, producing General John Stark Vodka, which went on the market in 2004.

Recognizing that not all grapes can survive the drastic New England winters, Frank Jr. and Linda decided to grow six varieties of grapes that can thrive in the area, including the North American hybrid Niagara, the American hybrid Cayuga, and French hybrids such as Maréchal Foch and Vignoles.

During the 2002–2003 season, the winter was especially harsh, and Flag Hill did not have a very productive grape harvest. Determined to continue wine production, the staff experimented with fruit wines, starting with apple cranberry, raspberry, strawberry, and Italian plum. These were so well received that Frank Jr. and Linda expanded to include blueberry and peach. Today, Flag Hill Winery produces delicious grape, fruit, and dessert wines, and New Hampshire's first port.

Flag Hill uses some fruit purchased from other areas, but hopes eventually to use only New Hampshire-grown fruit in their wines. Next on their agenda is sparkling wine.

Flag Hill Winery and Distillery features tours, tastings, and an idyllic setting for picnics or relaxing strolls. They have a wonderful on-site dining room with a menu spotlighting local ingredients, paired with Flag Hill wines. They also offer cooking classes featuring recipes made with Flag Hill wines and spirits.

Frank Jr. and Linda are always looking for ways to improve their beloved vineyard. Flag Hill has become the first in New Hampshire to get a glycol chiller, which will enable them to control a wine's temperature during the fermentation process, resulting in a product of consistent quality.

## CAYUGA WHITE

**2007**
NEW HAMPSHIRE
A bright semi-sweet and fruity white wine.

## MARECHAL FOCH

**2006**
NEW HAMPSHIRE
A dry red wine with the deep color of the French-hybrid grape.

## APPLE CRANBERRY FRUIT WINE

This silver medal winner contains 12.1 percent alcohol. A crisp, refreshing wine, comprised of 35 percent apple from Apple Hill Farm in Concord, New Hampshire, and 65 percent cranberry from Massachusetts. This wine offers a dry apple finish with a burst of tart cranberries.

## CAYUGA WHITE

Designed at Cornell University for the cold climate conditions of New York's Finger Lakes region, Cayuga grapes are extensively grown there. This hybrid is a cross between Seyval Blanc and Schuyler. This bright semisweet white, which is similar to a Riesling, is the most popular white wine at Flag Hill. The staff plans to use these grapes to create a sparkling wine in the near future.

## VIGNOLES

This is made from French hybrid grapes similar to Vidal. The vines are hardy and have tight cluster grapes, compact and perfect for making dessert wines. These grapes, which are susceptible to Botrytis rot in humid conditions, grow well in New Hampshire. This wine has a sweet, flowery bouquet with clean, crisp, sweet pineapple notes and agreeable acidity.

## WILD BLUEBERRY FRUIT WINE

This bright, semisweet fruit wine is made from wild Maine blueberries. This is a favorite for picnics and enjoying New Hampshire summers.

## MARÉCHAL FOCH

This grape is named after the French marshal Ferdinand Foch, who played an important role in the negotiation of the armistice terms during the closing of the First World War. The deep red color of the juice is said to signify the bloodshed by General Foch. Another French hybrid, this grape is one of the hardiest and most disease resistant. Most of the red Flag Hill produces is "Foch." Some believe the North American parent is really Oberlin Noir, a Gamay-riparia cross. Whatever the true genealogy, Maréchal Foch is often considered to possess Beaujolais characteristics, having the same sort of vibrant color, with berry fruit characteristics.

## NORTH RIVER PORT

New Hampshire's first port wine. The Flag Hill staff uses Maréchal Foch to make this deliciously elegant port. Technically, it is a tawny port, since it spends four to five years in oak, but it feels like a ruby port. It is wonderfully balanced with flavors of licorice, clove, and a touch of oak.

## CHERRY GLAZE

1 pound fresh cherries, pitted
¼ cup sugar
1 cup water
¼ cup Flag Hill North River Port
½ teaspoon ground allspice
1 teaspoon balsamic vinegar
Pinch salt and freshly ground pepper
2 tablespoons cornstarch

## PORK TENDERLOIN

One 1¼-pound pork tenderloin
1 bunch Swiss chard, chopped
2 small onions, julienned
1 tablespoon chopped garlic
2 teaspoons salt
1 teaspoon black pepper
3 to 4 tablespoons olive oil

SERVES 3 TO 4

# Cherry Glazed Kellie Brook Farm Pork Tenderloin

For the cherry glaze, combine the pitted cherries, water, and sugar in a saucepan and bring to a boil. Cook for 5 to 10 minutes, until the fruit is completely softened. Purée the mixture in a food processor or blender and strain through a fine mesh sieve. Bring the cherry sauce back to a boil with the allspice, vinegar, and port. Thicken, if you wish, by combining the cornstarch with ½ cup cold water and whisking it into the boiling cherry sauce. Season with salt and pepper and simmer 5 minutes, stirring frequently.

Sauté the onions in olive oil until soft and translucent. Stir in the garlic and Swiss chard and continue to cook until the chard is wilted. Cool the vegetables until ready to stuff the pork.

Trim the fat and sliver the skin from the tenderloin. Butterfly it open and lightly pound both sides. Season with salt and pepper. Fill the tenderloin evenly with cooled vegetables and roll it back together. Tie with butcher's twine. Grill the tenderloin over medium-to-high heat while basting with the cherry glaze. (Be careful not to burn off the butcher's twine.) Grill about 12 minutes or until a meat thermometer reaches 145°F. Let rest for 5 minutes before slicing.

Pour any remaining sauce over the sliced tenderloin, arrange on a platter, and serve.

2 tablespoons olive oil

1 whole chicken

4 ounces bacon, diced

1 large onion, diced

¾ pound mushrooms, quartered

2 cloves garlic, chopped

2 cups Flag Hill Apple Cranberry wine

4 cups chicken stock

1 tablespoon fresh thyme, chopped

2 tablespoons fresh parsley, chopped

¾ cup dried cranberries

1 tablespoon salt

½ tablespoon black pepper

SERVES 3 TO 4

Apple Cranberry Fruit Wine

# Coq au Vin

Cut the chicken into eight pieces and season with salt and pepper. Sear in a heavy-bottomed pan with olive oil. Remove the chicken to a plate. Render the bacon in the pan. Sauté the onions until soft and translucent. Stir in the garlic and mushrooms. Cook for 3 to 5 minutes, until the mushrooms are soft. Return the chicken to the pan and deglaze with wine. Cook about 2 minutes, then add the stock. Bring to a boil and add the herbs and salt and pepper. Simmer for 1 hour. The chicken is done when it's falling-off-the-bone tender.

Taste the broth and add a few more ounces of wine if it needs more tartness. Stir in the dried cranberries and adjust the seasoning to taste with salt and pepper.

1 pound elk medallions (*loin or round*)
1 small onion or shallot, diced
2 teaspoons salt
2 teaspoons black pepper, coarsely ground
2 to 3 tablespoons olive oil
¾ cup Flag Hill Wild Blueberry Wine
1 cup beef stock
½ teaspoon fresh thyme
¼ cup dried blueberries
4 tablespoons butter

SERVES 3 TO 4

Wild Blueberry Wine

# Velvet Pastures
# Elk au Blueberry Poivre

Season the elk medallions generously with salt and pepper. Sear the medallions in a heavy-bottomed skillet over high heat. Turn once after 2 minutes. Cook only to medium-rare, about 4 to 5 minutes total. Reduce the heat and remove the medallions to a platter.

Over medium-low heat, sauté the onions until soft and translucent. Deglaze the pan with Flag Hill Blueberry Wine. Increase the heat and reduce by half. Pour in the beef stock, thyme, and dried blueberries; bring to a boil. Simmer for 5 minutes and remove from heat. Finish the sauce by swirling in the butter until it is incorporated. Taste the sauce and adjust as needed with more salt and pepper. Pour the sauce over the elk medallions and serve.

# Jewell Towne Vineyards

Peter Oldak, MD, has been called the grandfather of New Hampshire's wine industry. This nickname refers not to his age, but rather to his owning New Hampshire's oldest operating vineyard.

Peter's interest in wine was sparked when, as a teenager, he read *The Wines of France*. By the time he started medical school, he was a member of Les Amis du Vin in Washington, where he studied wine and took classes. He completed his medical residency in Sonoma, California, which boasted about twenty vineyards at the time. The emergency room physician and his wife, Brenda, moved to South Hampton, New Hampshire, in 1977 and bought the Jewell Towne property.

At the time, they simply wanted to have a garden of their own. Peter planted a few grape vines in 1982, and in 1985 started making wine in his basement. A ravenous reader, he taught himself about viticulture. Medicine, which involves both chemistry and discipline, proved an excellent segue into winemaking.

In the early 1990s, Peter owned the northernmost winery in New England, and carefully studied the signature grapes of the Northeast. He bought vines from Philip Wagner, who founded Maryland's best-known winery, Boordy Vineyards, and introduced new varieties of French hybrid grapevines to America. Starting with more than sixty grape varieties, Peter soon narrowed down to about twenty types of grapes that he knew could survive cold New Hampshire winters and ripen in the short summers. Everything but "Bordeaux reds" did well, French-American hybrids especially. Today, he grows a variety of hybrids, including Aurore, Seyval, Vidal, Vignoles, Maréchal Foch, Léon Millot, Landot Noir, Chancellor, Baco Noir, and Rougeon. His *Vitis vinifera* varieties include Chardonnay, Gewürztraminer, and Pinot Noir.

In 1994, Peter released his first forty cases, which sold out in three weeks. Today, Jewell Towne produces ten thousand gallons per year, with the potential for twice that. From the beginning, this endeavor has been a family business. Brenda designs the wine labels and their two sons worked at the vineyard until they left for college. The family feels very fortunate to be able to work together at their beloved vineyard.

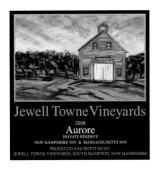

### Seyval

This wine is somewhat like a French Chablis, with an off dry, clean taste boasting melon, pear, and citrus flavors. It has good acid and a soft mouthfeel and is labeled 50 percent New Hampshire and 50 percent Massachusetts. This is the flagship white of Jewell Towne Vineyards.

### Aurore

This white hybrid grape variety, originally produced by Albert Seibel in 1860, is commonly used for wine production. Over a long lifetime, Seibel produced many complex hybrid crosses of *Vitis vinifera* to American grapes. The wine blends sweet and tart for a fresh young drink with a great mouthfeel.

### South Hampton White

This wine is a blend of every muscat Jewell Towne grows. It has a great nose of pineapple, orange rind, and pink grapefruit. As with all of their wines, it is stainless steel fermented. Sometimes they use oak chips for the benefits of oak without the barrels. This wine is also labeled 50 percent New Hampshire and 50 percent Massachusetts.

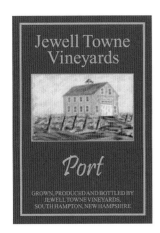

### Léon Millot

This grape is the offspring of a North American *Riparia-rupestris* and *Vinifera* (Goldriesling) parents. A Burgundy-like red wine with rich deep garnet color and round approachable tannins, with subtle aromas of cranberry, black raspberry, and licorice. Once used in the north of France as a blending wine to give color to Pinot Noir. It is an excellent food wine.

### Rhapsody in Blue

This amazing dessert wine is made with the Vidal grape, and the 2008 vintage tells an interesting story of perseverance. Bees ate $10,000 worth of the Vidal grapes at the end of the season, and Jewell Towne was left with only enough crops to produce about sixty bottles. The name is based on Peter's love for classical music, and the wine is a lovely composition. Its deep golden color is just the beginning of this romance in a glass.

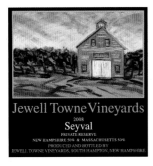

### New Hampshire Port

Chancellor is the primary grape for this unique port. It is not fortified; instead, they ferment it twice to raise the alcohol level to about 19 percent. Cigar-tobacco sweetness combines with chocolate and vanilla.

## Rhubarb Tomato Soup

RHUBARB TOMATO SOUP

¼ cup olive oil

4 stalks rhubarb, leaves removed,
    washed and chopped into ½-inch slices

1 stalk lemongrass, chopped
    as small as possible

1 ounce fresh ginger, peeled and minced

2 carrots, peeled and diced

2 stalks celery, diced

1 large red onion, diced

4 cloves garlic, peeled and minced

1 pound Roma tomatoes, quartered
    lengthwise and squeezed (to remove seeds)

2 tablespoons tomato paste

1 cup Jewell Towne Vineyards Aurore

2 quarts vegetable stock

3 tablespoons honey

Salt and cayenne pepper, to taste

CURRIED CHÈVRE

¼ cup chèvre

½ teaspoon curry

1 teaspoon honey

1 bunch fresh dill

SERVES 6

# Rhubarb Tomato Soup

### with Curried Chèvre and Dill

In a nonreactive heavy-bottomed stockpot, simmer the rhubarb, carrots, celery, and onion in olive oil for about 5 minutes. Add lemongrass, ginger, garlic, and tomatoes and simmer for 5 more minutes. Season with salt and cayenne pepper, add the tomato paste, and stir. When the vegetables begin to stick to the bottom of the pot, stir in the wine. Cook off the wine and add the vegetable stock. Bring to a boil, reduce to a simmer, and add the honey. Simmer for 10 minutes, or until all the components are completely soft. Remove from the burner and let cool for 20 minutes. Purée the soup in a blender while still a bit warm, adjusting the seasoning as needed.

Force the soup in batches through a fine mesh strainer or, preferably, a chinois, using a ladle to press out all the juice. The yield should be six bowls of velvety-smooth soup.

To make the curried chèvre, combine all the ingredients except the dill and mix until fully incorporated and consistent in color. You can serve this soup hot or cold, garnished with curried chèvre and snipped dill leaves.

CRANBERRY FENNEL PORK SAUSAGE

4-foot-length hog casings

2 pounds ground pork

8 ounces fatback or lardo, chopped small

6 cloves garlic, minced

1 tablespoon fennel seed, dry toasted
  and coarsely ground

2 tablespoons dried cranberries

1 cup Jewell Towne Vineyards Léon Millot

½ teaspoon ground allspice

2 sprigs fresh rosemary, chopped

2 tablespoons fresh sage, chopped

1½ tablespoons salt

½ teaspoon cayenne pepper

1 teaspoon dark chili powder

Healthy pinch pink curing salt (optional)

BRAISED BACON FRENCH LENTILS

1 cup French du Puy lentils

4 ounces smoked slab bacon,
  chopped into ½-inch cubes

3 large shallots, minced

1 carrot, diced small

1 stalk celery, diced small

1 tablespoon tomato paste

2 cups chicken stock (preferably low sodium)

1 teaspoon fresh tarragon leaves, chopped

1 teaspoon fresh Italian parsley, chopped

Salt and pepper

SERVES 8

# Cranberry Fennel Pork Sausage

## with Braised Bacon French Lentils

For the sausage, put on a pair of latex gloves. Soak the cranberries in the wine for 15 minutes. Then press the excess wine out of the reconstituted cranberries and, in a metal mixing bowl, knead all the ingredients except the casings until thoroughly combined. Refrigerate the bowl for at least half an hour.

Meanwhile, rinse the casings inside and out and fit them one at a time on a meat grinder sausage attachment. Force the chilled meat mixture into the casings and twist off 6-inch sausages as you go. These sausages will keep for several days. Store them in a refrigerator, uncovered, on a towel. Ideally, you should smoke the sausages, but if that is not possible, grill them on a covered grill over a hardwood fire.

For the lentils, rinse and place in a medium saucepan with a teaspoon of salt and plenty of water and bring to a boil. Reduce to a simmer and let cook for 15 minutes. Drain the lentils and set them aside. Meanwhile, in the same saucepan, render the bacon cubes and pour off most of the fat, leaving a tablespoon in the pan to sweat the cut vegetables with a little olive oil. Simmer the vegetables and bacon for 10 minutes. Stir in the tomato paste, salt, and pepper. Add the lentils and chicken stock and bring to a boil. Reduce to a simmer and let cook until all liquid has cooked off. Make sure the lentils are fully cooked. If not, add some water to the pan and simmer until they are soft.

Slice and fan the sausage on the bed of lentils and garnish with fresh herbs. Best served with whole-grain mustard.

1½ cups all-purpose flour
2 teaspoons baking powder
¼ teaspoon salt
½ teaspoon cardamom
5 tablespoons butter, room temperature
¾ cup brown sugar
2 eggs
⅓ cup canola oil
1 orange, zest only
1 lemon, zest only
1½ teaspoons vanilla extract
4 plums, halved and pitted
8 greengage plums, halved and pitted
   (*if unavailable, substitute with
   fresh prune plums*)

SERVES 8 TO 10

# Cardamom Plum Cake

Sift the flour and baking powder into a mixing bowl. Stir in the salt and cardamom.

In a mixer with a paddle attachment, beat the butter and brown sugar until light and creamy. Add the zest, eggs, oil, and vanilla and combine well. Add the flour mixture and combine again, until the batter is just uniform. Pour the batter into a buttered and floured 9-inch cake or springform pan—a springform pan is much easier to unmold. Place the halved plums flat-side-down on the surface of the batter in whatever pattern you like, being sure to leave some of the batter's surface exposed.

Bake in a preheated 375°F oven for 1 hour, or until the cake is golden-brown.

This cake makes a great pairing with Jewell Towne Vineyards New Hampshire Port.

# LaBelle Winery

Amy LaBelle is the perfect example of someone who has successfully followed her passions. As a corporate attorney for more than twelve years, she always loved wine and enjoyed dabbling with winemaking at home. When Amy traveled to Nova Scotia in July of 2001, she tasted blueberry wine for the first time and had a "lightening bolt" moment. Although she held a successful position as an attorney at Fidelity Investments in Boston, that blueberry wine made her realize that she wanted to run her own winery. While driving around Nova Scotia, she started developing a business plan. She returned home to Boston, read about winemaking, and committed to her dream.

On 9/11, she had to temporarily evacuate her condominium in Boston. Frightened and unsure at the time of what was happening, she packed only the essentials—which included her beloved first gallon of wine, which she had made out of nine pounds of blueberries.

Having successfully bottled blueberry wine, Amy expanded her efforts and started making peach, cranberry, and apple varieties—all in her 600 square foot Boston condo. In 2007, Amy moved to Amherst, New Hampshire, and, with the support of her family, got serious about winemaking. She opened LaBelle Winery and made four hundred cases in her first year. Today, she produces approximately 1,800 cases, or 24,000 bottles, of wine annually.

Amy now runs her winery out of a beautiful custom-built barn behind her Amherst home. Her husband Cesar helps make the wine and manage business operations. Their hope is to have their adorable young son Jackson assisting them someday.

LaBelle Winery uses New England fruits to make their wines, including apples from Alyson's Orchard in Walpole, New Hampshire, and cranberries from Massachusetts. They are committed to making wine from local fruits and vegetables within a short drive of their vineyard. They try to use only biodynamic and organic products.

Amy is also a talented chef, and has produced recipes for each of her wines. Her products are delicious to drink and great for cooking. She has created a tomato wine and an onion wine, and plans to produce a garlic wine—though her friends and family are not looking forward to peeling all that garlic. Her creative winemaking is inspiring.

### SEYVAL BLANC
This wine is dry with a perfect balance of acidity. The initial taste is of citrus, lemon in particular, and then a delightful mandarin orange fills the palate for a long, dry, clean finish. Delectable!

### HEIRLOOM APPLE
The mouthfeel of an apple is apparent in this wonderful wine, made with apples from Alyson's Orchard in New Hampshire. Imagine biting into a crisp, fresh-off-the-tree heirloom apple and then falling into a bed of roses and tulips—the feeling of summer!

### DRY APPLE
This dry apple wine is also produced using apples from Alyson's Orchard. It has a Chardonnay nose that gives way to a crisp, fresh low-acid wine. This is perfect for sangria *(see page 61)*, or as an apéritif before any meal.

### CRANBERRY
This bronze medal winner is made exclusively from New England cranberries, and is a wonderful option to serve on your next girls' night. The sweet-tart freshness would be great in a Cosmo!

### BLUEBERRY
This wine tastes like fresh, summer blueberries. It's made with 100 percent New Hampshire blueberries and aged slightly in French oak. Mild tannins give way to a lovely sweetness reminiscent of blueberry cobbler.

### JALAPEÑO PEPPER
Wow! This spicy wine is not for the faint of heart. This silver-medal winner is best used in chili, sauces, and guacamole. It gives a delicious "kick" to foods. Amy has a scrumptious chili recipe *(see page 63)* using this unusual wine as an ingredient.

4 tablespoons sugar

3 ounces apple or apricot brandy or
   peach schnapps

1 pint berries

1 lime, sliced

1 lemon, sliced

1 apple, sliced

2 ripe peaches or nectarines, sliced

1 bottle LaBelle Winery
   Dry Apple Wine (750 ml)

1 cup high-quality orange or
   passion fruit juice

Sparkling soda water

Serves 4 to 5

# Apple Wine Sangria

This sangria takes 5 to 10 minutes to assemble in a large pitcher, preferably one made of clear glass to show off the beautiful colors of the fruit. Prepare it a few hours ahead so the sangria has time to develop its fruity flavor.

For this recipe, you can use whatever fruits are in season and beautiful, so be creative! The more color, the better.

Combine all the ingredients but the soda water in a large pitcher. Chill the sangria several hours. When ready to serve, add soda water to the pitcher. Spoon fruits from the pitcher into glasses or goblets, adding a few fresh berries in each glass; pour the sangria over the fruit.

1 tablespoon olive oil

2 large red onions, chopped

3 tablespoons chopped jalapeño peppers
with seeds

6 garlic cloves, chopped

2½ pounds ground beef (*10% fat*)

1 tablespoon flour

4 tablespoons chili powder

2 tablespoons ground cumin

1 teaspoon salt

1 teaspoon paprika

1 can diced tomatoes, with juice

1 cup LaBelle Winery
Jalapeño Pepper Wine

Two 15-ounce cans kidney
beans, drained

One 14-ounce can beef broth

1 teaspoon cayenne pepper (*optional*)

Serves 6

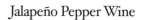 Jalapeño Pepper Wine

# Rustic Spicy Chili

## with Jalapeño Pepper Wine

Heat the oil in a large heavy pot over medium-high heat. Add the onions and sauté until translucent. Add the jalapeños and garlic and sauté for 1 minute. Add the beef and sauté until brown, breaking it up as it cooks, about 5 minutes. Add the flour, chili powder, cumin, salt, and paprika, then mix in the tomatoes with juice, LaBelle Jalapeño Pepper Wine, beans, and broth and bring to a boil. Reduce heat and simmer until the chili thickens, stirring occasionally, about 45 minutes. Kick up the heat with a little cayenne pepper, if desired. Can be made ahead; keep refrigerated and reheat before serving. Serve with optional toppings such as sour cream, grated cheese, green onions, tortilla chips, and cilantro.

SEYVAL BLANC RISOTTO

6 cups chicken broth

2 tablespoons butter

1 tablespoon olive oil

2 shallots, finely diced

1½ cups Arborio rice

1½ cups LaBelle Winery Seyval Blanc

2 tablespoons freshly grated
    Parmesan cheese (or chèvre, if you prefer)

Splash heavy cream

Salt and freshly ground pepper, to taste

PAN-SEARED SEA SCALLOPS

12 U-10 jumbo dry pack sea scallops

1 tablespoon butter

1 tablespoon olive oil

2 tablespoons flour

½ cup LaBelle Winery Seyval Blanc

Juice of ½ lemon

Salt and freshly ground pepper, to taste

SERVES 4

# Pan-Seared Sea Scallops

## with Seyval Blanc Risotto

In a saucepan, heat the chicken broth and let it simmer, covered, over low heat. In another saucepan, melt 1 tablespoon of the butter and the olive oil. Add the shallots and cook on low until translucent, just a couple of minutes. Add the rice and stir to coat in butter and oil. Toast the rice over medium heat, stirring constantly, for 4 minutes. Add LaBelle Winery Seyval Blanc and simmer, stirring, until the liquid is almost gone. Add 1 cup of the chicken stock and stir constantly until almost completely absorbed by the rice. Continue to add the warm broth 1 cup at a time, allowing each cup to be absorbed before adding the next. This will make the rice tender and creamy. Turn off the heat and add the remaining butter, cheese, heavy cream, and salt and pepper to taste.

For the scallops, melt the butter and olive oil in a pan at high heat and add the scallops, coated in flour. Do not move the scallops for about 4 minutes. Turn the scallops when you see the flour has formed a golden-brown crust. Once you have seared the other side, add the Seyval Blanc and the lemon juice and allow them to reduce and evaporate. Turn off the heat and add salt and pepper to taste.

This dish is great served with wilted spinach seasoned with nutmeg, salt, and freshly ground pepper.

# Piscassic Pond Winery

Roberta Gerkin and Nathan Smith, owners of Piscassic Pond Winery, started making honey wines for their own personal consumption, and enjoyed their hobby so much that they turned it into a career. Their winery, located on New Hampshire's Seacoast, is named after Piscassic Pond, a picturesque locale depicted on their original labels. Roberta and Nathan, who work out of their Newfields home, were granted licensing for their business in 2002 and made their first sale in 2004. Originally offering sixty bottles per year, they now produce about four hundred bottles annually.

This winery only produces honey wines, or mead wines, also called melomel or Metheglin. Mead, one of the oldest alcoholic drinks, is made from honey, water, and yeast. Mead can occur naturally, and was likely discovered as honey dripped from beehives and collected in pools of rainwater. Wild yeast consumed the sugar, producing a mildly alcoholic drink. Historically, many cultures referenced fermented honey beverages, especially during celebratory times.

Piscassic Pond Winery produces custom-crafted honey wines that are dry to semisweet, most with a light floral bouquet. Makers of mead enjoy a process free from worries like timing for harvest, pruning, thinning, and fermentation, which are all crucial elements of grape wine production. The Piscassic team produces three traditional meads, two spring meads (Vanilla and Rosehip), and one each of summer (Elderberry), fall (Pumpkin), and winter (Spiced) meads, fully celebrating all four seasons of the year.

The traditional meads are straightforward, made with honey, water, and yeast, but they vary in sweetness. The most traditional mead is a semi-dry (with similar sugar content to a Chablis); Léttsaett is lightly sweet (similar to a Reisling); and Hálfsaett is semisweet (not as sweet as a dessert or ice wine, but close). These should be served cold.

The Vanilla and Pumpkin meads are variations on the lightly sweet traditional mead. They are both great when served cold, but the Pumpkin is also delicious when heated. The Winter Spice is semisweet with mulling spices and should be served warm.

The Elderberry and Rosehip varieties are based off the semi-dry traditional, and are best served cold. The Elderberry is light and fruity, and though it is only offered seasonally, they may soon make this a year-round option because it is so popular. The Rosehip, as its name suggests, is floral, and pairs well with dark chocolate and cheesecake.

For people who find the flavor of mead to be a bit strong, it mixes well with apple cider, white grape juice, and cranberry juice. Piscassic Pond Winery features a certain number of bees on each bottle of wine to indicate the level of sweetness, enabling customers to select bottles according to preference.

*Piscassic Pond Winery*

*Léttsætt Traditional Mead*

Produced and Bottled by
Piscassic Pond Winery L.L.C. Newfields, NH

*Piscassic Pond Winery*

*Hálfsætt Traditional Mead*

Produced and Bottled by
Piscassic Pond Winery L.L.C. Newfields, NH

*Piscassic Pond Winery*

*Winter Spiced Mead*

Produced and Bottled by
Piscassic Pond Winery L.L.C. Newfields, NH

### ELDERBERRY MELOMEL

The driest of the meads, with a brick-orange hue like the color of a fine aged red wine. The dry fruit up front gives way to a slightly spicy finish. This wine could replace a favorite rosé on a hot summer day.

### LÉTTSAFTT TRADITIONAL MEAD

"Léttsaett" is Icelandic for "lightly sweet" and reflects the Nordic origins of this style of mead. It is deliciously golden in color and just mildly sweet at first taste. The floral notes taste like honey fresh from the beehive.

### HÁLFSAETT TRADITIONAL MEAD

Icelandic for "semisweet." This is similar to a dry German Riesling and would be great chilled as an apéritif or served with spicy dishes. It has a fresh, clean finish with just the right amount of floral beeswax.

### HONEY WINE WITH PUMPKIN AND SPICES

This dry mead can be served chilled or warmed. It smells and tastes like pumpkin-spiced cheesecake, and would be a lovely mead to serve for the holidays.

### ROSEHIP MELOMEL

The amber color resembles a fine sherry, and the nose has beautiful floral notes. It tastes like a well-made Madeira or dry sherry. A great apéritif!

### WINTER SPICED MEAD

This is a terrific option on a cold evening. Heat it, sip it, and warm up instantly. It is boldly spiced with cinnamon, clove, nutmeg, and orange zest.

Elderberry Melomel

## SWEET POTATO HASH

2 sweet potatoes, peeled and
    diced ½ inch
2 roasted poblanos, diced
1 small Spanish onion, sliced
1 red bell pepper, diced
2 cloves garlic, chopped
1 small jalapeño, diced
2 tablespoons chopped cilantro
1 teaspoon dried thyme
One 15-ounce can chickpeas, drained
    and rinsed
Salt and pepper, to taste

## PINEAPPLE MANGO CHUTNEY

½ pineapple, peeled and diced ¾ inch
1 large mango, peeled and diced ¾ inch
½ cup sugar
1 clove garlic, chopped
1 teaspoon crushed red pepper
Pinch allspice
1 cup pineapple juice
Salt and pepper, to taste

## PAN-ROASTED CHICKEN BREAST

Four 6-ounce boneless chicken breasts
2 teaspoons canola oil
¼ cup butter
¼ cup Elderberry Melomel
1½ cups chicken stock
¼ cup fresh cilantro
Salt and pepper, to taste

SERVES 4

# Pan-Roasted Chicken

### with Sweet Potato Hash and Pineapple Mango Chutney

For the hash, cook the diced sweet potato in a pot of boiling water until tender but not fully cooked. Drain and cool. Combine the remaining ingredients with the cooled sweet potatoes. Reserve at room temperature until ready to serve. About 10 minutes before the chicken is cooked, heat 2 tablespoons of butter over medium-high heat, add the hash mixture, and sauté until lightly browned and heated through.

To make the chutney, combine all the ingredients in a small nonreactive saucepan. Bring to a boil, reduce the heat, and simmer until the fruit is tender. Reserve at room temperature.

For the pan roasted chicken, heat the oil and 1 tablespoon of the butter in a 12-inch sauté pan over medium-high heat. Season the chicken with salt and pepper, then place in the heated pan. Cook for about 6 minutes, or until golden-brown. Turn and cook until the juices run clear when pierced with a knife, about another 6 minutes. Pour off any excess oil. Deglaze the pan with wine and reduce by half. Add the chicken stock and continue cooking until the liquid is reduced by half again. Remove the pan from the heat and swirl in the remaining butter and the cilantro.

Divide the sweet potato hash onto serving plates. Top with the chicken breasts and pan sauce. Spoon the chutney over the chicken.

## SPICED HONEY WINE CIDER GLAZE

2 cups Piscassic Pond Winery Honey
   Wine with Pumpkin and Spices
2 cups apple cider
1 bay leaf
2 medium shallots, chopped
4 sprigs thyme
4 whole black peppercorns
2 tablespoons butter

## ROCK SHRIMP RISOTTO

2 quarts chicken stock
3 tablespoons olive oil
1 pound Arborio rice
1 small Spanish onion, diced
2 cloves garlic, finely chopped
1 cup Piscassic Pond Winery Honey
   Wine with Pumpkin and Spices
1 cup cooked rock shrimp
½ cup cooked diced butternut squash
1 teaspoon lime zest
1 medium jalapeño, sliced thin
2 tablespoons chopped cilantro
Salt and pepper, to taste

## SEARED SALMON

Four 6-ounce salmon fillets
2 ounces olive oil
Salt and pepper, to taste

## WATERCRESS AND PICKLED GINGER SALAD

2 bunches watercress, cleaned
Pickled ginger, to taste
Splash olive oil
Salt and pepper, to taste

SERVES 4

Honey Wine with Pumpkin and Spices

# Seared Salmon with Spiced Honey Wine Glaze

## with Rock Shrimp Risotto and Watercress Pickled Ginger

For the glaze, combine the first six ingredients in a nonreactive saucepot over medium heat. Reduce until one cup of liquid remains. Strain into a small saucepan and whisk in the butter. Hold at room temperature until ready to serve.

For the risotto, bring the chicken stock to a boil, then reduce the heat to low. In another saucepot, heat the oil over medium heat, add the onions and garlic, and cook until the onions are softened. Add the rice, stirring with a wooden spoon for 7 to 10 minutes. Add Piscassic Pond Winery Honey Wine with Pumpkin and Spices and continue stirring until absorbed. Ladle 1 cup of the simmering chicken stock into the rice. Cook for 2 minutes, stirring continuously, until the stock is almost completely absorbed. Repeat, 1 cup of stock at a time, until all is absorbed. The rice should be firm yet cooked through in about 20 minutes total cooking time. Gently fold in the rock shrimp, butternut squash, lime zest, cilantro, and jalapeño. Keep warm until ready to serve.

For the salmon, season the fillets with salt and pepper on both sides. Heat the oil in a 12-inch sauté pan over medium-high heat. Cook the salmon for about 3 to 4 minutes, until lightly caramelized, then turn and cook for 3 minutes longer. Reduce the heat and cook for another 3 minutes, until the salmon is opaque in the center.

Combine the watercress and ginger in a small bowl, toss with oil, and season with salt and pepper.

POACHED PEAR

4 Bartlett pears, peeled
4 cups Piscassic Pond Winery
   Hálfsaett Traditional Mead
2 cups granulated sugar
4 whole black peppercorns
1 bay leaf
½ cinnamon stick
4 whole allspice berries
2 ounces fresh ginger, sliced

PUFF PASTRY

1 sheet puff pastry dough
2 tablespoons granulated sugar
1 teaspoon cinnamon
4 tablespoons melted butter

MANGO AND PINEAPPLE ICE CREAM

6 egg yolks
¾ cup granulated sugar
1 pint whole milk
1 cup heavy cream, chilled
1 teaspoon vanilla extract
Pinch salt
3 ounces dried mango
3 ounces dried pineapple

SERVES 4

Hálfsaett Traditional Mead

# Poached Pear and Crispy Cinnamon Puff Pastry

### with Mango and Pineapple Ice Cream

For the poached pears, place all ingredients except the pears in a large nonreactive saucepan and bring to a boil. Place the pears in the liquid and cover. Lower the heat and simmer until the fruit is tender and cooked all the way through. Remove and cool. Strain the remaining liquid into another pan and gently reduce until it reaches a syrup-like consistency. Reserve in a warm spot until ready to serve.

Lay the puff pastry dough on a lightly floured work surface. Brush the dough with melted butter and sprinkle with sugar and cinnamon. Using a biscuit cutter, cut the dough into circles and place on a parchment-lined cookie sheet. Bake in a 375°F oven until the dough is golden-brown and crispy. Reserve at room temperature until ready to serve.

To make the ice cream, combine the egg yolks and sugar in a bowl. Whip until thick and light. Scald the milk and gradually beat it into the egg mixture. Heat the mixture over a water bath, stirring constantly, until it thickens. Remove from heat. Stir in the cold cream to stop the cooking. Add the vanilla and salt, then chill the mixture overnight. Gently fold in the dried fruit and store in the freezer until ready to serve.

# Zorvino Vineyards

Jim Zanello worked in the electronic packaging industry, collected cars, and enjoyed woodworking as a hobby until a new barn, a trip to California, and a small crop of grapes changed his life.

Jim originally bought his Sandown, New Hampshire, property to store his vast car collection and provide space for his woodworking endeavors. Needing a covered building to protect his cars, he hired contractors to build a barn. While his barn was under construction, he visited California, where he toured wine country and enjoyed his first "taste" of the wine industry.

Once the barn was completed, people started asking if they could hold parties in the space. Jim turned the barn into a function facility and eventually sold his cars.

Shortly thereafter, he went to Italy, where his ancestors had lived, and fell in love with the culture. He was inspired by the Italians' passion for good food, wine, and friends, and vowed to embrace a similar lifestyle. He planted a few vines of Valiant grapes to try making wine for himself. Before this first crop was even ready, he had decided to start his own winery. Zorvino Vineyards was established in 1999.

The winery's name came from Jim's original family name, Zorzanello, which was shortened to Zanello when the family came to America. He combined the "Zor" from his original surname with the Italian word for wine, "vino," to create "Zorvino." The first grapes he purchased were Carménère, Malbec, and Chardonnay, which he used to produce eight hundred cases of wine. Today, the vineyard produces 2,500 cases annually.

Jim added a crop of Niagara grapes, and considers the Niagara and Valiant varieties to be his "hobby" vines. He makes thirty to forty cases a year using these grapes, which he combines to make 100 percent Sandown-grown Rosso.

In the spring of 2008, Jim planted St. Croix, Frontenac, Frontenac Gris, and La Crescent grapes. It takes about three years before a vine can produce any usable fruit, and the peak crops are harvested during years six through twenty. Jim also planted peaches and raspberries, which he plans to use to make 100 percent New Hampshire fruit wines. Zorvino strives to be as local as possible, and their goal is to produce more Sandown-grown varieties. While they wait for crops to mature, Zorvino Vineyards is using local peaches and apples, and cranberries from Massachusetts. They also use grapes from California and Chile.

Jim is not the sole winemaker at Zorvino; he now has the help of Ken Evers and Tom Zack. New Hampshire wine enthusiasts can look forward to sampling this vineyard's exciting new wines in the years to come.

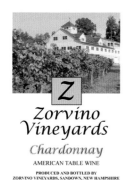

Zorvino
Vineyards
*Chardonnay*
AMERICAN TABLE WINE
PRODUCED AND BOTTLED BY
ZORVINO VINEYARDS, SANDOWN, NEW HAMPSHIRE

Zorvino
Vineyards
*Cabernet Sauvignon*
AMERICAN TABLE WINE
PRODUCED AND BOTTLED BY
ZORVINO VINEYARDS, SANDOWN, NEW HAMPSHIRE

Zorvino
Vineyards
*Malbec*
AMERICAN TABLE WINE
PRODUCED AND BOTTLED BY
ZORVINO VINEYARDS, SANDOWN, NEW HAMPSHIRE

### SAUVIGNON BLANC

This wine is made from the juice of Chilean grapes, and is the beautiful golden color of Chardonnay. While drinking this wine, you will taste an explosion of tropical fruit and pineapple.

### RESERVE CHARDONNAY

This Chardonnay spent one year in the bottle. It is very crisp and balanced, with hints of banana and toasted chestnuts. They do not use any oak for this Chardonnay, but it does spend some time "sur lie," or on the lees, which is the leftover sediment and yeast, giving it a nice, soft mouthfeel.

### PEACHEZ

This 2008 bronze medal winner is made with 100 percent New Hampshire peaches and tastes like summer breezes. The fresh peach offers mouth-watering zest and acidity, with the perfect amount of fruitiness.

### ZINFANDEL

This wine is brambly with a nose of blackberry spice. The weight of the wine is comparable to skim milk, and would be a perfect accompaniment to barbecues.

### CABERNET SAUVIGNON

The fruit for this wine depends on the time of year you buy a bottle. For instance, the bottles available in the fall of 2008 were made from South American fruit from the 2008 harvest. In the spring of 2009, they will use grapes from California from the 2008 harvest. This is a young wine, and the flavors and body continue to develop nicely. The color is very light, and the taste is bursting with fresh blueberry and plum. This Cabernet will appeal to Merlot drinkers.

### MALBEC

A very jammy yet bold red. They soak medium-toast oak chips for about six months in this South American juice. They only produce about two hundred cases, so grab it when you can.

Two 8-ounce fresh tuna steaks
2 avocados, peeled and diced into
    ½-inch pieces
¼ pound cherry tomatoes
1 cup panko crumbs
Fresh focaccia bread
¼ cup mayonnaise
1 lime, zest only
2 tablespoons cooking oil
12 sprigs cilantro, coarsely chopped
Salt and pepper, to taste

SERVES 4

Sauvignon Blanc

# Seared Tuna and Avocado

## with Fresh Focaccia Bread

Pat the tuna steaks dry and then press them into the panko crumbs to coat lightly. Heat the cooking oil in a skillet until very hot and sear the tuna steaks on each side for 20 to 30 seconds. Remove from the pan and let rest. In a large mixing bowl, combine the avocados, mayonnaise, zest, cilantro, and tomatoes. Slice the tuna into ½-inch squares and add to the mixture. Season with salt and pepper and toss gently. Slice the focaccia bread and grill on each side. Spoon the tuna over the focaccia slices and serve as an appetizer, or over mixed greens as a light salad. Also excellent in a baguette as a sandwich! This dish makes a great pairing with Zorvino Vineyards Sauvignon Blanc.

Two 6-ounce Chilean sea bass fillets

1 large baking potato

1 large red onion, diced

1 cup Arborio rice

¼ pound asparagus, chopped into
    ½-inch pieces

1 cup heavy cream

2 cups chicken stock

½ cup balsamic vinegar

3 tablespoons cooking oil

¼ cup Parmesan cheese

2 tablespoons brown sugar

3 tablespoons vegetable oil

Zest of 1 lemon

1 sprig fresh rosemary, chopped

Splash Zorvino Vineyards
    Reserve Chardonnay

Salt and pepper, to taste

SERVES 4

Reserve Chardonnay

# Potato Wrapped Chilean Sea Bass

## with Red Onion Relish and Lemon Asparagus Risotto

For the risotto, heat 2 tablespoons of cooking oil in a medium-sized saucepan. Add the Arborio rice and toss until lightly browned. Splash with Zorvino Vineyards Reserve Chardonnay and add salt and pepper, lemon zest, and chicken stock. Bring to a boil. Reduce the heat and simmer until the water is absorbed, about 15 to 20 minutes. Let stand for 5 minutes, then return the pan to the burner and fold in the heavy cream, Parmesan cheese, and chopped asparagus. Stir the mixture over low heat until it achieves the desired texture, no more than 1 to 2 minutes.

For the red onion relish, dice the red onion and sauté in cooking oil over medium-high heat. Add the brown sugar, chopped rosemary, and balsamic vinegar. Reduce until almost all the liquid is gone and the onions are transparent. Set aside.

For the Chilean sea bass, slice the potato thinly lengthwise, about ¹⁄₁₆ of an inch, and lay 2 to 3 slices lengthwise overlapping one another. Take the sea bass and roll it in sliced potato, covering most of fillet, then dredge in flour. Heat an oven safe frying pan to high heat, then sear the fish in 1 tablespoon of oil until brown on each side, about 30 seconds per side. Transfer to a preheated oven at 425°F for 12 to 15 minutes, depending on the thickness of the fish.

To serve, spoon the relish over the sea bass, with a side of risotto, and accompany with Reserve Chardonnay.

12-ounce breast of veal

½ pound penne (*or your favorite pasta*)

¼ pound cremini mushrooms, sliced

4 slices prosciutto

6 eggs, beaten

2 balls buffalo mozzarella, egg-sized and
   sliced in half

1 cup heavy cream

¼ cup brandy

¼ cup tomato juice

2 tablespoons garlic cloves, chopped

2 tablespoons cooking oil

4 fresh basil leaves

1 cup flour

Fresh parsley

Parmesan cheese, freshly grated

Salt and pepper, to taste

SERVES 4

# Veal Bocconicini

## with Fresh Penne

Slice the veal thinly into four equal portions, about 3 ounces each. Pound the medallions to flatten them, lay out, and roll each with a basil leaf, mozzarella slice, and prosciutto slice, then roll in flour and dip into the egg batter. Heat the cooking oil to medium-high heat in an oven safe frying pan, add half of the garlic, and lightly brown the rolled veal on each side. Then splash with brandy. (Warning: the brandy may ignite!)

Next add the heavy cream, sliced cremini mushrooms, remaining garlic, and tomato juice and bring to a boil. Top with grated Parmesan, then place in the oven at 400°F for 10 to 12 minutes or until the sauce is reduced by one-third. Meanwhile, boil water and prepare the pasta as directed.

To serve, loosen the rolled veal in the pan, then spoon over your pasta. Sprinkle with grated Parmesan, fresh-snipped parsley, and salt and pepper. Accompany with a glass of Malbec.

# The Wineries

Candia Vineyards
702 High Street
Candia, NH 03034
603.867.9751
candiavineyards.com

Farnum Hill Ciders
98 Poverty Lane
Lebanon, NH 03766
603.448.1511
farnumhillciders.com

Flag Hill Winery and Distillery
297 North River Road
Lee, NH 03861
603.659.2949
flaghill.com

Jewell Towne Vineyards
65 Jewell Street
South Hampton, NH 03827
603.394.0600
jewelltownevineyards.com

LaBelle Winery
100 Chestnut Hill Road
Amherst, NH 03031
603.828.2923
labellewinerynh.com

Piscassic Pond Winery
38 Oaklands Road
Newfields, NH 03856
603.778.0108
piscassic.com

Zorvino Vineyards
226 Main Street
Sandown, NH 03873
603.887.8463
zorvino.com

# Glossary

**Acid:** One of the five tastes of wine. Can be felt on the back sides of the tongue, like biting into a green apple.

**Botrytis:** A mold found on grapes causing the grape to shrivel, concentrating and intensifying both sugar and flavor, also known as "noble rot". Necessary to make wines like Sauternes.

**Bouquet:** The fragrance a wine releases due to fermentation and aging.

**Decanting:** A process used to either let a wine breathe and open up, or to filter out sediment.

**Fermentation:** Yeast eats the sugar and creates alcohol and carbon dioxide. Grape juice becomes wine.

**Finish:** The flavor and feel of the wine left on the palate after the wine is swallowed.

**Fortified Wine:** The process of adding brandy or alcohol to a wine, stopping the fermentation process and increasing the alcohol percentage. Used for wines like Port and Madeira.

**Foxy:** A musky, earthy, or grapey quality found in wines made with grapes from the North American vine species *Vitis labrusca*.

**Glycol Chiller:** Recirculating temperature control system. Allows the control of fermentation temperatures to induce a particular flavor from the juice.

**Hybrid:** Hybrids are created in an effort to produce a vine with the best traits of its parents. In challenging environmental conditions this will give a vine more productivity, disease resistance, and better adaptability.

**Lees:** Dead yeast cells and sediment separated from the wine after fermentation.

**Malic Acid:** One of the three primary acids in wine. The along with tartaric and citric. Malic acid is found in fruits and vegetables; one of the richest source is apples.

**Reserve:** A term used to indicate a better quality of wine although it has no legal significance in the United States.

**Ruby Port:** A fortified wine which is aged in wood for about two years. The wine is bottled while it still exhibits youth, fruitiness, and a bright red color. Ruby ports are generally the least expensive.

**Sommelier:** The French term for a wine steward or person in charge of the wine service. Certified Sommeliers pass an exam given by the Court of Master Sommeliers.

**Sulfites (sulfur dioxide):** A preservative used in winemaking and grape growing. Some people complain of being allergic to sulfites when studies have shown that only 1 percent of the population truly has a sulphite allergy. All wines contain sulfites. Yeast naturally produces sulfites during fermentation so there is only a rare wine which contains none.

**Sur Lie:** "On the lees." Stirring the lees with the juice to give more body and complexity to the wine.

**Tannins:** The phenolic compounds caused by skins, seeds, and stems in red wine and barrel aging in white wines. The feeling of sandpaper down the middle of the tongue. Tea and walnuts are also very high in tannins.

**Tawny Port:** A fortified wine made from a blend of grapes from several different years. Aged in wood for as long as forty years. Lighter and softer than ruby port tawny in color.

**Viniculture:** The study and science of winemaking.

**Viticulture:** The study and science of grapes, vines, and grape growing.

**Vintage:** The date the grapes were harvested. If there is no date on the bottle, then the wine is a blend of grapes harvested from different years.

**Vitis labrusca:** A native North American grape species, responsible for the foxy character described in some wines.

**Vitis riparia:** A native North American vine species known for its resistant rootstock and breeding hybrids.

**Vitis vinifera:** A native European grape species. Some of the best known are Cabernet Sauvignon, Chardonnay, Sauvignon Blanc, Merlot, and Pinot Noir.

**Yeast:** Cultivated or natural microscopic, single-celled organisms essential for the fermentation process and developing the flavors and aromas in wine.